This edition published in the UK in 2018

ISBN-13: 978-1727102833 (createspace assigned)

ISBN-10: 1727102835

MeEducation   Website: **meeducation.net**

Please feel free to contact the author at - **meeducation@yahoo.com**

Other books by the same author:

- **English Vocabulary Builder 1**
- **English Vocabulary Builder 2**
- **English Vocabulary Builder 3**
- **English Vocabulary Builder 4**
- **Idioms In English**

Acknowledgements

The author would like to thank the following colleagues, friends and family for their help and support during the writing and production of this publication:

Andrada Melinte, Maciek Sarara, Sihao Zhou, Dahira Khalid, Irene Koukeli, Erika Evans, Mitsue Kinoshita and Kaneko Harada.

Mark Evans has been a teacher for over 25 years. He has taught in Australia, Japan, Malaysia and the UK. He graduated in languages from University College London and has a PGCE, CELTA, DELTA, Additional Diploma in ESOL, as well as an MA in English Language Teaching. He currently lives in London where he teaches at a college and a university.

Speaking Grammar: Table of Contents

Lesson Plan for Speaking Grammar Course

Tutor:	Topic (circle):		Date:
	Present Simple; Present Continuous; Present Simple & Present Continuous; Past; Question Forms; Indirect Questions; Present Perfect; Present Perfect Continuous; Past Perfect; Future; Narratives; Future Continuous & Future Perfect; Comparatives & Superlatives; Modals of Obligation; Modals of Deduction; Gerunds & Infinitives; Conditionals; Mixed Conditionals; Wish/If Only; Have Something Done; Quantifiers; Relative Clauses; So and Such; The Passive; Reported Speech; Reporting Verbs; Definite Articles; Prepositions; Used to; Phrasal Verbs – Get; Phrasal Verbs – Go.		

Time	Content	Tutor Activity	Student Activity
5	Ice breaker	T displays questions about grammar topic on IWB. T checks answers.	Ss discuss questions in pairs.
15	Focus on form	T elicits form. T elicits rules of target grammar use. T provides handout. T asks for examples.	Ss provide form. Ss provide rules. Ss give examples of target grammar.
15	Grammar exercise	T does first question with ss & tells them to do rest.	Ss tell T answer to first question. Ss do exercise. Ss check answers in pairs.
5	Exercise check	T checks answers with ss & goes through any problem areas.	Ss tell T answers & ask for further explanation if required.
15	Speaking	T explains activity. T gives model answers to provide ss with ideas.	Ss discuss with partner while T monitors.
5	Feedback & Consolidation	T asks individuals what they talked about ensuring they use target language. T recaps grammar point & usage.	Ss provide feedback to T.

Unit 1: Present Simple

FORM: I/You/We/They **play**; He/She/It **plays**

NEGATIVE: I/You/We/They **don't** play; He/she/It **doesn't** play

1) Habits/routines
2) States
3) Timetable future

Change the verbs into to the correct form and put in the gaps:

1) Martin _____ going for a run in the park (love).

2) Sarah _____ her colleagues at work every day (meet).

3) Kevin _____ well at night because of the noise (sleep).

4) She _____ by train every weekday (travel).

5) Ralph _____ his neighbour anymore (like).

6) That's such a nice shirt, Ed. You _____ so smart (look).

7) Kenny _____ beer at a bar every night (serve).

8) Every night Dave _____ Italian food in a restaurant (cook).

9) I really like my new job. I _____ about it every day (think).

10) Karen _____ a cup of coffee every morning (drink).

11) Ethel _____ sick. She can't work for a while (feel).

12) Because I have a bad back, I _____ anymore (work).

13) My new job _____ at 7 o'clock tonight (start).

14) Alfred _____ very hard as he wants to pass his exams (study).

15) Frederick _____ his car anymore (drive).

Speaking Practice

Put the words in the correct order then ask your partner:

1) every/what/you/do/do/day?

2) time/what/get/you/morning/every/up/do?

3) go/bed/to/what/do/time/you?

4) often/do/how/you/use/computer/a?

5) shopping/where/go/you/do?

6) take/you/do/bath/shower/or/night/at/a?

7) you/how/relax/you/do/tired/are/when?

8) how/go/out/often/eat/to/a/in/restaurant/you/do?

9) do/how/to/you/school/get/work/or?

10) you/eat/and/what/every/do/drink/day?

11) often/you/how/friends/do/your/meet?

12) do/friends/what/your/you/do/meet/when/you?

13) you/do/meet/who/often/most?

14) do/like/what/holiday/you/on/doing?

15) free/what/do/like/you/when/are/you/doing?

Extension – make at least 5 more present simple questions to ask your partner:

Unit 2: Present Continuous

FORM: I **am** (not); You/We/They **are** (not); He/She/It **is** (not)+ **Verb + ing**
1) Actions happening now
2) Future arrangements (know time & place)

Change the verbs into the appropriate form and put in the gaps:

1) Don't go outside because it _____ very heavily (rain).

2) What _____ you _____ now (do)?

3) The little girl _____ because she lost her toy (cry).

4) Matthew _____ because he is so nervous (shake).

5) I _____ bad because I have a stomach ache (feel).

6) You _____ really _____ me by asking silly questions (irritate).

7) Simon _____ as a cleaner at the moment (work).

8) I _____ my friend in a park this afternoon (meet).

9) Ken and Billy _____ at university anymore (study).

10) Sorry but the computer _____ at the moment (work).

11) When _____ you _____ your holiday from work (take)?

12) The phone _____. I'll answer it (ring)!

13) I'm upset as my English _____ fast enough (improve).

14) Robert _____ tomorrow at 8 o'clock in the morning (work).

15) The business _____ quickly and is taking on more staff (grow).

16) Ben _____ in the marathon next week (run).

17) Nick _____ training at his company next week (do).

18) I feel a little sad when the sun _____ (shine).

Speaking Practice

Put these words in the right order to make questions:

1) you/are/what/now/doing?

2) living/where/you/are/now?

3) going/where/you/are/weekend/next?

4) who/meeting/next/are/you/week?

5) friend/what/doing/now/is/your?

6) next/holiday/where/you/are/going/your/for?

7) friend/where/living/now/your/is?

8) are/eating/what/you/tonight?

9) friend/where/your/is/working/moment/the/at?

10) thinking/about/moment/the/are/at/you/what?

Extension – write at least 5 more questions to ask your partner:

1)

2)

3)

4)

5)

Unit 3: Present Simple & Present Continuous

What is the difference between "he watches TV" and "he is watching TV"?

Present Simple:

FORM: I/You/We/They **walk**; He/She/It **walks**
1) Habits/repeated actions
2) States
3) Timetable future

Present Continuous:

FORM: I **am**; You/We/They **are**; He/She/It **is** + **Verb** + **ing**

1) Actions happening now
2) Future arrangements (know time & place)

Change the verbs into to the appropriate tense and put in the gaps:

1) Tom _____ TV in the living room now (watch).

2) She _____ her friends at the cinema tonight at 8 (meet).

3) Steve _____ playing football in the park (love).

4) He _____ to central London by train every day (commute).

5) It _____ anymore so we won't get wet (rain).

6) What a lovely dress, mum. You _____ fantastic (look).

7) Bill isn't here right now. He _____ beer with a friend (drink).

8) The show _____ at 6 o'clock tonight (start).

9) I _____ about my girlfriend every day (think).

10) He _____ about buying a new house (think).

11) Dave _____ under the weather. He wants to go home (feel).

12) She _____ lasagne in the kitchen now (cook).

Speaking Practice

Rearrange the words to make questions. When you have finished, ask and answer with your partner:

1) nights/do/Saturday/you/what/do/on/usually?

2) usually/weekends/how/your/do/you/spend?

3) restaurant/often/do/how/out/a/go/in/to/you/eat?

4) are/what/now/doing/you?

5) going/where/you/are/tomorrow?

6) travel/work/do/to/how/or/you/school?

7) you/meet/how/your/often/friends/do?

8) book/you/at/what/reading/are/the/moment?

9) participating/are/in/any/at/you/activities/moment/clubs/the/or?

10) learning/to/how/anything/are/the/do/you/at/moment?

Extension - write at least 5 more questions to ask your partner:

Unit 4: Past Simple (Regular)

Positive	Negative	Question
I watch**ed**	I **didn't** watch	**Did** you watch?
He clean**ed**	He **didn't** clean	**Did** he clean?
We play**ed**	We **didn't** play	**Did** we play?

*BUT: <u>Usually</u> "**Y**" changes to "**i**" when you add "**-ed**"*

Study > stud**ied**   Copy > cop**ied**

*Change these words to the **past** then put them in the correct form in the gaps (some are negative):*

cook/watch/wash/relax/visit/dance/start/listen/clean/study/play/climb

1) She _____ a great film on TV last night.

2) Henry _____ his room even though it was filthy.

3) The lesson _____ on time because the teacher was late.

4) She _____ a delicious meal for the family dinner.

5) _____ Bill and Bob _____ English in the library?

6) They _____ the mountain while they were on holiday.

7) Susan _____ her parents at their home yesterday.

8) He _____ his clothes as his washing machine was broken.

9) _____ he _____ at the party last night?

10) Malcolm had a radio which he _____ to every day.

11) I _____ at home on the bed last night as I was exhausted.

12) Edward _____ tennis yesterday as he had a bad back.

Past Simple (Irregular)

These are all irregular – *put the past tense into the gaps:*

Verb	Past	Verb	Past	Verb	Past	Verb	Past
Buy		Go		Make		Sleep	
Can		Have		Meet		Speak	
Do		Is		Pay		Stand	
Drink		Know		Read		Take	
Eat		Leave		See		Write	

*First change these words to the **past** then put them in the spaces:*

meet/drink/go/speak/see/read/write/buy/pay/take/leave/do/eat/stand

1) I _____ to the park yesterday.

2) He _____ a cup of tea in the café last night.

3) They _____ fish and chips in the park by the river.

4) When she was on holiday she _____ a letter to her boyfriend.

5) She _____ to her sister on the phone for a long time.

6) He _____ all his friends at the pub last Saturday night.

7) Mary _____ a bottle of wine in the supermarket.

8) Linda _____ college late last night.

9) When I was in the park, I _____ a cat climbing a tree.

10) I _____ a lot of money for my new shoes.

11) I _____ on the bus because there were no seats.

12) Kevin _____ a great book last week.

13) As it was too late to walk home, he _____ the train instead.

14) Steve _____ his English homework before he slept.

Past Simple (Irregular)

For the 'be' verb, there is a special form:

Positive	Negative	Question
I/he/she/it **was**	I/he/she/it **wasn't**	**Was** I/he/she/it?
we/you/they **were**	we/you/they **weren't**	**Were** we/you/they?

Fill in the gaps with the correct form of the 'be' verb in the past:

1) As it was hot, there _____ many children swimming in the pool.

2) Where _____ you yesterday? I couldn't find you.

3) When I arrived the train _____ there. It had already left.

4) The people at the party _____ very friendly so I left as soon as I could.

5) She _____ only five years old when she learnt how to play the piano.

6) Do you know if he _____ happy when he met you?

7) Bernard _____ at home when the postman knocked at the door, so he left the parcel with a neighbour.

8) Although I looked for them, they just _____ there.

9) We _____ all delighted for him when he won the prize.

10) It _____ wet when we woke up but it is now.

11) Even though there was thunder and lightning, the little kitten _____ scared at all.

12) Kevin _____ sure if he had locked the door, so he had to go back home to check.

13) They _____ very happy when they dropped the expensive vase.

14) _____ he tired when he came home from work?

Speaking Practice

Talk about these topics in detail using the past tense:

Your life in your country.

Your childhood.

Your last job/school.

A holiday you had.

A good/bad meal you had.

A trip you had.

A happy/sad day.

Games you played when you were younger.

A good friend you had.

Unit 5: Past Continuous

FORM:
I/he/she/it **was (n't) + Verb + ing**
We/you/they **were(n't) + Verb + ing**

Use for a continuous action happening in the past

*Put the appropriate form of the **past continuous** into the gaps:*

1) When I woke up it _____ heavily (snow).

2) At 3 o'clock yesterday we _____ football (play).

3) I _____ when the doorbell rang (eat).

4) All the ladies _____ beautiful dresses to the ball (wear).

5) Tom injured his leg while he _____ in the park (exercise).

6) I bumped into a friend while I _____ in the queue (stand).

7) It _____ in the morning but it is now (rain).

8) While I _____ to catch my flight, I dropped my wallet (run).

9) She _____ along the street when she saw an accident (walk).

10) David saw some spectacular sights while he _____ on his trip around the world (travel).

11) He _____ where he was going, so his car hit a tree (look).

12) Mary _____ on the bench when her sister called (sit).

13) They _____ in the maths lesson, so they didn't know how to do the homework (concentrate).

14) Burt _____ a new dish for his family when he realised that he didn't have all the ingredients (make).

Speaking Practice

Answer these questions with your partner:

1) What were you doing at 4am this morning?

2) What were you doing at 9am this morning?

3) What were you doing yesterday lunchtime?

4) What were you doing at 4pm yesterday afternoon?

5) What were you doing at 7pm last night?

6) What were you doing at 10pm last night?

7) What were you doing at midnight?

8) What were you doing at this time yesterday?

9) What were you doing this day last week?

10) What were you doing this time last month?

11) Where were you living last year?

12) What were you doing when it was raining last?

Complete these sentences:

1) When I was going to school/work, I...

2) When I was growing up, I...

3) While I was waiting for the bus/train, I...

4) I once fell asleep while I ...

5) I once had an accident while I...

6) When I was looking out the window, I...

7) When I was watching TV, I...

8) When I was travelling once, I...

Unit 6: Question Forms

For **present/past simple tenses** (not "*be*" verb):

Question word	Auxiliary verb	Person/thing	Infinitive	...
Where	does	she	live?	
How many pens	do	you	have?	
	Does	he	like	cats?
What	did	you	do	yesterday?
Where	did	she	go?	

For **present/past simple tenses** for "*be*" verb:

Question word	"be"	Person/thing	...
How	is	your mother?	
	Are	you	happy?
What	is	your country's	name?
Where	was	the city	you visited?
Who	were	they?	

Ask Tom questions about his life:

1) (Where/from) "_____?" "The UK."

2) (Where/live now) "_____?" "London."

3) (What/your hobby) "_____?" "Chess."

4) (How often/play) "_____?" "Every day."

5) (Married) "_____?" "Yes, I am."

6) (Children) "_____?" "Yes, I do."

7) (How old/they) "_____?" "3 and 5."

8) (What/wife do) "_____?" "She's a doctor."

9) (She/like her job) "_____?" "Yes, she does."

10) (How often/work) "_____?" "5 days a week."

Speaking Practice:

Make questions with these prompts then ask your partner:

1) Where/you/live? _____

2) Do/like/where/live? _____

3) Where/live/before? _____

4) When/born? _____

5) Where/born? _____

6) What/do? _____

7) How/get/to school/work? _____

8) Married? _____

9) Children? _____

10) How many brothers/sisters? _____

11) Who/like best in your family? _____

12) Who/best friend? _____

13) What/hobby? _____

14) How often/exercise? _____

15) What/do/last weekend? _____

16) Who/meet/last weekend? _____

Extension - write at least 3 more questions to ask your partner:

Question Forms 2

Write the questions to these answers and then ask your partner:

1) _____

I'm a student.

2) _____

I'm 27.

3) _____

I've lived here for two years.

4) _____

I've been learning English for about three years.

5) _____

Pizza.

6) _____

I like listening to pop music.

7) _____

My best friend is Ken.

8) _____

My friends would describe me as friendly.

9) _____

My dream is to have a big house.

10) _____

Meeting friends makes me happy.

Extension – make at least 3 more questions to ask your partner:

Unit 7: Indirect Questions

Which is correct: "Do you know what time it is?" or "Do you know what is the time?"

Why do we use indirect questions?

Rules:
1) word order: Subject > Verb
2) use "**if**" for yes/no questions
3) don't use auxiliary verbs (do/does/did)

Convert these to indirect questions:

1) Where is the bank? > Could you tell me...

2) Who are you? > Would you mind telling me...

3) Why was he late? > Can you tell me...

4) Where were you? > Would you mind informing me...

5) What is that? > Do you know...

6) How can I do it? > Could you teach me...

7) Were you early? > Would you mind telling me...

8) How much is it? > Do you have any idea...

9) Did you do it? > Can you inform me...

10) What did you see? > Could you tell us...

11) Where does he live? > Have you any idea...

12) Who did you meet? > Would you tell us..

13) Are you satisfied? > Could you tell me...

14) Did he meet him? > Can you inform me...

Speaking Practice

Put these words in the correct order to make questions then ask your partner:

1) where/the/can/tell/me/you/train/is/station/nearest?

2) you/can/me/how/get/to/inform/to/station/the?

3) where/you/do/know/best/the/eat/city/your/to/in/place/is?

4) you/know/way/a/money/good/do/make/to?

5) idea/any/you/who/man/richest/the/the/world/is/do/have/in?

6) me/tell/about/you/where/can/live/you?

7) me/could/way/a/a/you/tell/job/good/get/to?

8) child/tell/would/about/you/when/me/were/you/a?

9) know/house/country/much/how/you/do/costs/your/in/a?

10) tell/you/what/best/place/country/the/your/is/in/could/me?

11) informing/mind/me/way/what/a/good/you/would/English/learn/is/to?

12) me/how/this/in/long/country/live/going/to/are/you/you/could/tell?

Extension – write at least 5 more indirect questions to ask your partner:

Unit 8: Present Perfect

What is the difference between "I ate breakfast this morning" and "I have eaten breakfast this morning"?

What is the form of the present perfect?

When do we use the present perfect?

FORM: **Person + have/has (not) + PP**

1) Time bridge between past and present

2) Experience

3) Use with: *just, yet, already* and *for* & *since*

---

*Put the verbs into the appropriate form, **past** or **present perfect**:*

1) She _____ a shower twice today (take).

2) They _____ him four days ago (meet).

3) John _____ where he left his bike last week (forget).

4) She _____ there for three months now (live).

5) Ken _____ so much since I last saw him (grow).

6) I _____ time to eat my dinner yet (have).

7) Where's Tom? He _____ out but he'll be back soon (go).

8) Ray _____ his best friend for ten years (know).

9) Sophie _____ some money and handed it in to the police (find).

10) I studied French at college. However, now I _____ it (forget).

11) Tina _____ away for a week but she came back yesterday (go).

12) I can't see my car. It _____ over there. It _____ (be, steal).

Speaking Practice

Rearrange the words to make questions and when you have finished ask and answer with your partner:

1) have/what/done/you/today?

2) long/for/how/here/have/lived/you?

3) just/done/what/you/lesson/have/the/before?

4) for/long/best/friend/have/your/how/known/you?

5) already/today/have/eaten/you?

6) most/life/bought/what/the/is/thing/expensive/your/you/in/whole/have?

7) done/is/what/the/have/exciting/most/life/you/your/ever/in/thing?

8) the/ever/what/seen/is/best/film/you/have?

9) you/met/have/person/who/the/is/strangest/ever?

10) is/beautiful/where/have/the/you/most/visited/place/ever?

11) eaten/is/you/the/what/best/food/have/ever?

12) received/the/what/best/have/is/present/birthday/ever/you?

13) country/the/best/where/your/is/to/place/you/been/have/in?

14) you/which/to/talk/place/about/have/a/been/yet/not/can/you?

Extension – write at least 3 more questions to ask your partner:

Unit 9: Present Perfect Continuous

What are the uses of the present perfect continuous?

What is the form?

FORM: **Person + have/has (not) + been + V –ing**

1) Action started in past and still continuing

2) Continuous action in past which has recently finished but the results can be seen now

NB The verbs *live* & *work* can be in present perfect or present perfect continuous without changing the meaning

---

*Fill in the blanks using **present perfect** or **present perfect continuous**:*

1) I _____ English for three years now (study).

2) Tom's hands are filthy. He _____ football in the park (play).

3) You look exhausted! What _____ you _____ (do)?

4) Linda _____ five letters today (write).

5) I feel dizzy as I _____ wine all afternoon (drink).

6) Sue _____ from a heavy cold for a fortnight (suffer).

7) They _____ tennis twice this week (play).

8) Someone _____ all my beer. There is none left (drink).

9) Jill and Jim _____ for three years now (go out).

10) Your eyes are red. _____ you _____ (cry)?

11) The room is clean now. It _____ (clean).

12) My bike is OK now. Tom _____ it (fix).

Speaking Practice

Rearrange these words to make sentences (do not make them into questions!):

Talk about...

1) a/a/that/hobby/have/doing/been/for/you/time/long.

2) learning/long/how/have/you/English/been.

3) long/how/been/you/here/living/have.

4) frequenting/an/a/have/for/that/time/you/been/long/establishment.

5) following/TV/have/a/been/programme/you.

6) a/you/of/music/have/that/listening/been/kind/to.

7) good/a/you/been/have/friend/visiting.

8) shop/a/you/while/going/been/for/have/a/to.

9) a/have/reading/you/been/that/book.

10) have/long/your/you/job/been/how/doing.

Write at least 5 present perfect continuous questions to ask your partner:

1)

2)

3)

4)

5)

Unit 10: Past Perfect

When do we use the past perfect? What is the form?

FORM: **Person + had (not) + PP**
Use about a past event which happened before another past event

Past perfect is *not usually* used if:
1) the sequence of events is clear: "I ate breakfast and went to work."
2) we use with two past simple verbs and the first action is just before the second: "When we got there, we started eating."

---

*Fill in the gaps with the appropriate tense, **past simple** or **past perfect**:*

1) When Johnny woke up, he realised that everyone _____ (leave).

2) By 6pm everyone in the office _____ home (go).

3) Later he found out that his cat _____ at the same moment (die).

4) He clambered into bed and _____ straight away (sleep).

5) The hotel staff cleaned the room as soon as the guests _____ (leave).

6) Dibner visited the field where she _____ as a child (play).

7) After having arrived home, Maggie noticed that she _____ her purse in the pub (leave).

8) They looked around and _____ their friend in the corner (see).

9) Bernard _____ his classmate for over ten years (meet).

10) Peter reminded me of the time when I _____ over (fall).

11) When he opened the door he immediately _____ his key (drop).

12) Though they were late, the show _____ yet (start).

Speaking Practice

Ask your partner these questions and add something extra:

When was the last time you...

were exhausted?	were scared?	felt optimistic?
felt pessimistic?	felt anxious?	felt blissful?
were embarrassed?	felt sad?	were injured?
(or your friend) called the police?	felt proud?	were in a bad mood?

What had happened/What had you done?

Unit 11: Future Tenses

What's the difference between "I'm going to meet Tom tonight" and "I'm meeting Tom tonight"?

What's the difference between "It's going to rain" and "It will rain"?

Present continuous - arrangements (you know the time & place)

Be going to + inf. - plans
- predictions (based on what you see/know)

Will + inf. - predictions (based on what you think)
- spontaneous decisions
- 100%
- promises
- offers

Shall is a formal version of will

Fill in the gaps with the most appropriate form of the future:

1) It's dark in here. I _____ the light (turn on).

2) England is playing very well. At this rate they _____ (win).

3) I _____ tomorrow at 8 in the morning (work).

4) Brendan _____ TV tonight (watch).

5) The phone's ringing. I _____ it (answer).

6) The Titanic has hit a large iceberg. It _____ (sink).

7) I promise I _____ you tonight (call).

8) Tom has bought his plane ticket. He _____ tomorrow (leave).

9) I _____ my new dress to the party (wear).

10) That shelf looks very precarious. It's _____ down (fall).

11) It's Jane's birthday tomorrow. She _____ 27 (be).

12) I _____ you a lift in my car to the station (give).

Speaking Practice:

Rearrange these words to make questions about the future. When you have checked, ask and answer with your partner and add more information:

1) you/are/tomorrow/what/doing?

2) you/what/do/going/to/weekend/the/at/are?

3) tomorrow/time/are/what/up/you/get/to/going?

4) are/shopping/when/you/going/go/to/next?

5) will/marry/ever/a/do/foreigner/you/think/you?

6) think/who/win/will/you/World/do/next/the/Cup?

7) next/you/what/place/is/to/visit/the/are/going?

8) class/you/going/what/do/are/to/after?

9) think/ever/become/do/will/you/wealthy/you?

10) going/you/your/to/summer/spend/how/next/are/holiday?

11) like/you/do/what/think/be/tomorrow/will/weather/the?

12) next/person/are/to/you/meet/is/the/who/going?

Extension – make at least 3 more questions:

Unit 12: Narrative Tenses

What are the four narrative tenses?
What are the forms of the four tenses?
What are the advantages of learning narrative tenses?

---

1) Past simple tense – finished action in past with no connection to present
FORM: **Person + V + ed**

2) Past continuous tense – continuous action in past
FORM: **Person + was/were V + ing**

3) Past perfect tense – finished action in past that occurred before another past action
FORM: **Person + had + PP**

4) Past perfect continuous – continuous action in past that occurred before another action in past
FORM: **Person + had + been + V + ing**

Past Simple V Past Continuous

Fill in the blanks with the appropriate form of ***past simple*** *or* ***past continuous***:

1) When I went to bed last night it _____ (rain).

2) It _____ every single day last week (rain).

3) I _____ the meal in the restaurant was delicious (think).

4) I asked her what she _____ about (think).

5) She _____ for twelve hours last night (sleep).

6) When I came back this morning the cat _____ (sleep).

7) The pupil _____ after she failed the exam (cry).

8) I saw a little girl who _____ in the park (cry).

9) A big house _____ on top of the hill (stand).

10) They _____ in the queue when it started raining (stand).

Past Perfect V Past Perfect Continuous

*Fill in the gaps with the correct form of **past perfect** or **past perfect continuous**:*

1) He _____ very hard for a long time before he died (work).

2) Although he was a chef, he _____ as a doctor before (work).

3) The man _____ for years before he was caught (steal).

4) She was ill as she _____ raw meat the night before (eat).

5) It _____ for three hours before he got up (rain).

6) The room stank. Jane _____ fish all morning (cook).

7) Steve was filthy; he _____ rugby in the park (play).

8) His skin was totally burnt; he _____ in the sun all day (sit).

9) They had to walk home as their car _____ (break down).

10) The cash _____ from the bar before the police came (steal).

Mixed narratives. The Journey.

Put the correct narrative form of the verbs in brackets into the spaces below:

When I _____ (wake) up the ground was all wet as it _____ (rain). I _____ (leave) my house to meet my friend Colin. We _____ (take) the train together to London. As the train _____ (leave) the station, I _____ (realise) that I _____ (forget) my passport. I _____ (get) off at the next station and _____ (return) home. When I _____ (get) home I _____ (look) for my passport. Just then I _____ (remember) that I _____ (give) it to Colin to look after! I _____ (take) a cab back to the station and Colin said that he _____ (forget) that I _____ (give) him my passport. We finally _____ (arrive) at the airport but our plane _____ already _____ (leave)!

Speaking Practice

Talk about these topics in detail using the narrative tenses:

A friend you met by chance.

A time when you saw a famous person.

The plot of a book you have read.

A holiday experience.

A wedding you have been to.

An embarrassing incident.

A stroke of bad luck.

A quarrel you have had with someone.

An incident at work.

Unit 13: Future Continuous & Future Perfect

When do we use these tenses?

What are the forms?

Future continuous:
FORM: **Person + will (not) + be + V-ing**
Action occurring at a future point in time

Future perfect:
FORM: **Person + will (not) + have + PP**
Action finished before a future point in time

---

*Fill in the gaps with either **future continuous** or **future perfect**:*

1) Tom _____ the same job when he's 20 (do).

2) I _____ the report by 5pm tonight (finish).

3) If you need to reach me I _____ my cousin (visit).

4) Sue hopes she _____ for a prestigious company by the time she's 30 (work).

5) By the time I am 40 I _____ to over 40 countries (travel).

6) Although the room is filthy now, it _____ by tonight (clean).

7) Do you think you _____ in this country next year (live)?

8) By next fortnight I _____ the film 5 times (see).

9) This time next week I _____ on a beach (sunbathe).

10) For sure, we _____ the meeting by midday (finish).

11) Next March Eliza _____ a teacher for 10 years (be).

12) When I'm 70 I hope I _____ my retirement (enjoy).

13) _____ you _____ here long (stay)?

14) Unfortunately, I _____ my work by the deadline (complete).

Speaking Practice:

Answer these questions and add something extra:

What will you be doing:

1) at 9pm tonight?

2) at midnight?

3) this time tomorrow?

4) this time next week?

5) this time next month?

6) in 5 years' time?

7) in 10 years' time?

8) in 50 years' time?

What do you hope you will have done:

1) by 10pm tonight?

2) by next weekend?

3) by the end of the month?

4) by the end of the year?

5) by the end of the decade?

6) by the time you are 60?

7) by the time you retire?

8) before you pass away?

Extension: make at least 3 more questions to ask your partner:

Unit 14: Comparatives and Superlatives

1) If one syllable, add "**–er/est**"… *kind>kinder>kindest*

2) If more than 1 syllable, add "**more/most**"… *more interesting*
BUT NOT if last letter is "**y**"… change "**y**" to "**i**" & add   "**-ier/iest**"
    happy>happier>happiest

3) If you have **consonant/vowel/consonant**, double the last letter…
big>bigger>biggest

4) **Irregular**:
Good>better>best   Bad>worse>worst   Far>further/farther>furthest/farthest

5) **(not) as…adjective…as** = the same…
London is as busy as Paris

Put the correct form of the adjectives in the gaps:

1) An elephant is much _____ than a mouse (big).

2) I live _____ away than Tom (far).

3) I'm happy as my life is _____ than before (interesting).

4) Steve is _____ at maths than me (bad).

5) This is the _____ food I have ever eaten (bad).

6) I was much _____ when I was younger (healthy).

7) Education these days is _____ as in the past (not hard).

8) He's feeling much _____ than before (good).

9) I don't live _____ away as I used to (far).

10) That is the _____ book I have ever read (boring).

11) A shark is far _____ than a fish (dangerous).

12) Andrada is _____ girl in Chigwell (intelligent).

13) A snail is _____ as a cheetah (not fast).

14) Gold is much _____ than lead (precious).

Speaking Practice

Compare these topics using comparative language and add extra information: eg "London is much bigger than my city."

1) Where you live now/your hometown.

2) The weather where you live now/your country's weather.

3) Your life here/life in your country.

4) Education here/education in your country.

5) Transport here/transport in your country.

6) Food where you live now/your country's food.

7) Your generation/your parent's generation.

8) Your country now/your country 20 years ago.

9) Your life now/your life when you were younger.

10) The environment now/the environment previously.

11) Healthcare where you are now/healthcare in your country.

12) Fashion now/fashion in the past.

13) The economy where you live now/the economy in your country.

14) Music now/music in the past.

15) People where you live now/people in your country.

16) Crime where you live now/crime in your country.

Extension – talk about other differences using comparative forms.

Unit 15: Modal Verbs of Obligation & Advice

What is the difference between "I must go now" and "I have to go now"?

What is the difference between "you should see a doctor" and "you must see a doctor"?

Present	Past
Have to + inf.(external obligation)	**Had to + inf.**
Must + inf. (internal obligation & written official rules)	**Had to + inf.**
Must not + inf.	**Wasn't/Weren't allowed to + inf.**
Don't have to + inf.	**Didn't have to + inf.**

Should (not) + inf. (advice)	**Should (not) have + PP**
Must (not) + inf. (strong advice)	----------------

Fill in the gaps with the most appropriate modal form:

1) My school was very strict. We _____ a school uniform (wear).

2) He has a headache. He _____ some aspirin (take).

3) You are seriously ill. You _____ to hospital immediately (go).

4) My boss has just called. I _____ the report right away (finish).

5) Read the sign! It says you _____ over 18 to see the film (be).

6) It's snowing. You _____ the house without a coat (leave).

7) When you're in Rome you really _____ the opera (visit).

8) I'm exhausted. I _____ now (leave).

9) When I was at school we _____ maths every day (study).

10) It looks like it's going to rain. You _____ an umbrella (take).

11) You _____ a tie if you don't want to (wear).

12) We _____ for the meal yesterday because John paid for it (pay).

Speaking Practice

Rules in your Country

Talk about the rules in your country using modal verbs (e.g. "You don't have to wear a school uniform in my country."):

1) Wear school uniform

2) Start school at 4 years old

3) Study hard

4) Drive on the left

5) Wear a seatbelt in a car

6) Get married in a church

7) Vote in elections

8) Take shoes off before you enter someone's house

9) Pay income tax

10) Have a license for a dog

11) Drink alcohol on public transport

12) Ride a bicycle on the pavement

13) Pay for your education

14) Stay at school until you are 18

15) Smoke in the workplace

Extension – talk about other rules in your country.

Unit 16: Modals of Deduction

What is the difference between "John might be 30" and "John must be 30"?

Must be	Might/Could be	Can't be
100% definite	50% true	100% impossible

(Don't use *can* for deductions!)

Put the most appropriate modal of deduction into the gaps:

1) Who's that at the door? It _____ Margaret; she's gone away on holiday.

2) You've been working all day! You _____ exhausted!

3) I'm not sure about the weather but I heard it _____ sunny tomorrow.

4) He's married with 2 kids and he finished university 3 years ago. He _____ at least 25.

5) She's not answering the phone. She _____ in the shower.

6) He's a bit slimmer than before. He _____ on a diet.

7) She _____ feeling under the weather. I saw her jogging in the park yesterday.

8) Linda _____ pregnant. She's got a large tummy.

9) She doesn't speak any English at all. She _____ British.

10) They look quite similar. They _____ twins.

11) Richard lives in a huge, fantastic house on the banks of the river. He _____ very wealthy.

12) I feel dizzy. I _____ coming down with the flu.

13) Bill has lost his passport and he's flying tomorrow. He _____ really worried.

14) You want me to lend you £10,000! You _____ serious!

Speaking Practice

Fact or Myth?

Discuss whether these statements are facts or myths using modals of deduction and give your reasons:

1) The most common name in the world is John.

2) Italians drink the most coffee per head in the world.

3) There are over 100 types of pasta.

4) Kissing is good for your teeth.

5) People in the US are the richest per head in the world.

6) Your teacher grows and shrinks during the day.

7) People in Iceland have the highest life expectancy.

8) Parts of your body grow after you die.

9) The Queen of England has two birthdays.

10) Saturn is the biggest planet in the solar system.

11) Women's hearts beat faster than men's.

12) Lachanophobia means the fear of vegetables.

13) Swiss eat the most chocolate per head in the world.

14) The US drinks the most coca cola per head in the world.

15) The dumbest dog in the world is a poodle.

16) An oyster can change its gender.

17) The average child asks more than 100 questions a day.

18) The word Spain means 'land of the rabbits'.

Unit 17: Gerunds & Infinitives

When do we use a gerund and when do we use an infinitive?

Gerunds (V-ing)	Infinitives (to + inf.)
Subject of a sentence	To show a purpose
After prepositions	After adjectives
After certain verbs: *discuss, dislike, don't like, enjoy, keep, practise, recommend, suggest.*	After certain verbs: *agree, choose, decide, hope, learn, refuse, tend, want.*

Put the verbs in the correct form, gerund or infinitive:

1) It's good _____ after a hard day's work (relax).

2) I enjoy _____ wine on a hot summer's day (drink).

3) _____ healthy food is good for you (eat).

4) He agreed _____ with his mother yesterday (go).

5) She finished her juice before _____ to the park (walk).

6) I recommend _____ that restaurant by the beach (try).

7) _____ fit is beneficial for both your mind and body (keep).

8) Tom refused _____ his dinner as it was inedible (eat).

9) She came to London _____ English at a language school (study).

10) They fell over after _____ too much (drink).

11) Jane discussed _____ a job in France for the summer (get).

12) I hope _____ a better job after I pass my exams (get).

13) They went to the supermarket _____ groceries (buy).

14) It was fantastic _____ my colleagues again after such a long time (meet).

Speaking Practice

Fill in the gaps with a gerund or infinitive. After checking, ask and answer these questions with your partner using a gerund or infinitive and add more information:

1) What job do you hope _____ in the future (do)?

2) What do you like _____ in your spare time (do)?

3) Do you enjoy _____ English (learn)?

4) How often do you practise _____ English (speak)?

5) Why did you decide _____ to this lesson (come)?

6) Where do you want _____ for your next holiday (go)?

7) What is the first thing you do after _____ up (get)?

8) What is the last thing you do before _____ to bed (go)?

9) Is _____ housework enjoyable for you or a chore (do)?

10) What sort of things stop you from _____ (sleep)?

11) Is _____ fit fun for you (keep)?

12) After a hard day, what do you think it is nice _____ (do)?

13) Is there anything you are worried about _____ (do)?

14) Where do you recommend _____ to for a holiday in your country (go)?

15) What is the best way _____ your English (improve)?

16) What do you tend _____ when you are bored (do)?

Extension: make at least 5 more questions to ask your partner:

Unit 18: Conditional Patterns

How many conditionals are there? What are the forms?

Can you give an example of each?

0) (100%/habits)	*If you heat ice, it melts* **If + present, present**
1) (50%)	*If it rains, I will bring an umbrella* **If + present, will + inf.**
2) (0.1%/hypothetical)	*If I won the lottery, I would buy a car* **If + past, would + inf.**
3) (0%)	*If I had known, I would have told you* **If + past perfect, would have + PP**

Zero and first conditional

*Fill in the blanks with a **0** or **1**st conditional (some are negative):*

1) If you _____ from a plane, you _____ (jump, die).

2) He will _____ if he _____ any extra money (resign, get).

3) If it _____, I _____ drenched (rain, get).

4) The door always _____ if you _____ the button (open, push).

5) If I _____ a lot of money, I _____ a house (win, buy).

6) If you _____ water to 100°C, it _____ (heat, boil).

7) Unless we _____, we _____ the bus (hurry, miss).

8) Be careful! If you _____ the cat, it _____ you (stroke, scratch).

9) I always _____ if people _____ me (blush, compliment).

10) Provided you _____, you _____ the exam (study, pass).

Second and third conditional

*Fill in the blanks with a **2nd** or **3rd** conditional form:*

1) If I _____ a bird, I _____ in the sky (be, fly).

2) If I _____ you, I _____ a new car (be, buy).

3) She _____ more attractive if she _____ nicer clothes (be, wear).

4) If Tom _____ better in the last job interview, he _____ the post (do, get).

5) If I _____ more money, I _____ a bigger house (have, buy).

6) If I _____ the company was going bankrupt, I _____ a long time ago (know, resign).

7) She _____ happier if she _____ in paradise (be, live).

8) If she _____ 1 minute earlier, she _____ you (arrive, see).

9) If his parents _____, he _____ born (meet, be).

10) If my bike _____ , I _____ the police (steal, notify).

Speaking Practice:

Write the questions to these answers:

1) Q: _____

A: If I won a lot of money….

2) Q: _____

A: If I go on holiday this year, I'll probably visit….

3) Q: _____

A: If it snows tomorrow….

4) Q: _____

A: If I spoke better English…

5) Q: _____

A: If my friend got into trouble…

6) Q: _____

A: If it's sunny…

7) Q: _____

A: If I could travel to the moon…

8) Q: _____

A: If someone pays me a compliment…

9) Q: _____

A: If I had been born 1,000 years ago…

10) Q: _____

A: If my wallet was stolen…

11) Q: _____

A: If someone of the opposite sex smiles at me…

12) Q: _____

A: If I ever emigrated…

Unit 19: Mixed Conditionals

What is a mixed conditional?

Past Condition > Present Result
If + past perfect, would + infinitive
If my parents hadn't met, I wouldn't be here

Present Condition > Past Result
If + past simple, would have + PP
If I was smarter, I would have got into university

Fill in the blanks with the appropriate mixed conditionals:

1) If I _____ harder, I _____ a rich man by now (work, be).

2) We _____ in London now, if we _____ our connecting flights (be, miss).

3) If I _____ more enthusiastic about learning English, I _____ a job as a translator (be, get).

4) If I _____ a good cook, I _____ you a nice meal last night (be, make).

5) If you _____ your atlas, we _____ lost now (forget, be).

6) We _____ late if our old car _____ down (be, break).

7) If he _____ every last penny, he _____ broke now (spend, be).

8) If he _____ faster, he _____ the race (be, win).

9) If Bob _____ studious, he _____ yesterday's test (be, pass).

10) I _____ here now if my parents _____ (be, meet).

11) He _____ so fat if he _____ so much food (be, eat).

12) If he_____ patient, he _____ the teaching job (be, get).

Extension – write at least 3 more mixed conditional sentences:

Speaking Practice

Rearrange these words to make questions then ask your partner:

1) would/if/where/hadn't/now/be/you/here/you/come?

2) doing/would/what/had/you/you/if/be/studied/harder/English/now?

3) had/you/if/born/poor/life/your/be/been/how/would/different?

4) would/were/how/you/if/feel/metre/you/taller/one?

5) you/if/were/you/what/would/clever/more/have/done?

6) would/you/if/have/done/what/were/you/invisible?

7) your/you/if/be/both/broken/had/legs/would/how/different/life?

8) if/a/would/you/were/good/what/cooked/cook/me/have/you?

9) you/if/lost/your/had/all/who/for/ask/would/money/you/help?

10) won/you/if/had/be/lottery/how/life/the/would/your/now/different?

Extension – make at least 5 more mixed conditional questions:

1)

2)

3)

4)

5)

Unit 20: Wish/If only

What is the difference between *wish* and *if only*?

What happens to the verb if you use *wish/if only*?

Fact: *"It is cold."*   Wish: *"I wish it was hot."*

Fact	Wish
Present	Past
Present continuous	Past continuous
Future (going to)	Was/were going to
Past simple	Past perfect
Past continuous	Past perfect continuous
Present perfect	Past perfect

Change the following from the facts to wishes:

FACT	WISH
1) I live in London.	I wish...
2) I am working tomorrow.	....
3) I'm going to meet my boss.	....
4) I didn't study at school.	....
5) I have left my girlfriend.	....
6) I was cooking all day.	....
7) I've broken my leg.	....
8) I'll be 40 next birthday.	....
9) I lost my job.	....
10) My car has been stolen.	....
11) My computer is broken.	....
12) No one listens to me.	....

Speaking Practice

Talk about your wishes and regrets and provide more information. (E.g. "I wish I had studied harder.") Is there anything you regret about:

1) your English?

2) your education?

3) your family?

4) the area where you live?

5) your house/flat?

6) your career?

7) your schooldays?

8) when you were younger?

9) your parents?

10) your finances?

11) a relationship?

12) your country?

13) your life in general?

14) your personality?

15) your diet?

16) a friend?

Extension – talk about any other regrets with your partner.

Unit 21: Have Something Done

FORM: **Person + have + object + PP**
e.g. I had my hair cut

1) Use when we arrange somebody else to do something for us
(Using "get" instead of "have" is informal)

2) Use when something (usually bad) happens to us or our
belongings

Fill in the gaps using the "have something done" structure:

e.g. My hair is getting long. <u>I am going to have it cut</u>.

1) My jacket is dirty. I'm _____ (clean).

2) John's house needs painting. He's _____ (paint).

3) Kim's TV is broken. She's _____ (fix).

4) I want earrings. I'm _____ my ears _____ (pierce).

5) Eri's hair is shorter now. She _____ (cut).

6) Now my roof is fixed. I _____ (repair).

7) Sue has no purse. She _____ (steal).

8) Have you ever _____ your luggage _____ by customs (search)?

9) I don't like _____ my picture _____ by anyone (take).

10) Ken has satellite TV. He _____ yesterday (install).

11) The wind broke my fence. I _____my fence _____ (blow down).

12) I didn't make my cake. I _____ by the bakery
(make).

Speaking Practice

Put these words in the correct order then ask your partner and add something more:

1) your/hair/cut/where/you/do/usually/have?

2) mind/having/photo/you/do/taken/your?

3) time/last/when/your/was/taken/photo/the/had/you?

4) you/your/money/stolen/have/ever/had?

5) cake/a/made/you/have/ever/had?

6) you/had/ears/your/pierced/have?

7) you/ever/had/anything/repaired/have?

8) ever/do/cleaned/dry/you/clothes/your/have?

9) you/do/fix/your/house/or/it/have/repaired/yourself/someone/by?

10) you/ever/had/part/body/of/have/a/your/broken?

11) time/last/had/you/homework/when/was/the/checked/your?

12) phone/broken/have/ever/you/had/your?

Extension - write at least 5 more questions to ask your partner:

1)

2)

3)

4)

5)

Unit 22: Quantifiers

What is the difference between "I drink a lot of wine" & "I drink lots of wine"?

Countable	A lot of/ lots of	(Not) Many	Plenty of	Several	A few
Uncountable	A lot of/ lots of	(Not) Much	Plenty of	-	A little

"A few" = not many   "Few" = less than expected (negative)

Put the most appropriate quantifier in the space below:

1) We don't have _____ time left.

2) There is only _____ wine in the glass.

3) There are _____ people living in my suburb as it's so popular.

4) It's important to drink _____ water every day.

5) I don't have _____ good friends who live near me.

6) Susan has only been to hospital _____ times in her life.

7) Come in and sit down! We have _____ room!

8) Do you have _____ relatives?

9) His house is expensive. He spent _____ money refurbishing it.

10) Bernard feels lonely as _____ of his friends live abroad.

11) After I got made redundant I only have _____ money these days.

12) I can only see _____ ducks swimming in the pond.

13) A: How much bread do you have? B: Not _____.

14) Can I just have _____ milk in my tea, please?

15) As he is so rude, _____ people like him.

16) When I'm cooking I only try to use _____ salt.

Speaking Practice

First, put these nouns into the correct boxes. Then, talk about them using appropriate quantifiers. E.g. Question: "How <u>much</u> water do you drink?" Answer: "I drink <u>a lot of</u> water" and add extra information.

water	sweets	alcohol	coffee
meat	vegetables	fish	bread
junk food	wholemeal food	fruit	games
TV	movies	dramas	game shows
sport	exercise	rice	health food

Countable	Uncountable	Both

Unit 23: Relative Clauses

What is a relative clause? What are the 2 types of relative clauses?

Defining Relative Clauses – give <u>essential</u> information
"He's the man who lives next door."

Non-defining Relative Clauses – give <u>extra</u> information
"The man, who is 27, lives next door."

* Don't' use *"that"* for non-defining relative clauses

Relative Pronouns:

Which – for things
Who – for people
That – for people & things
Whose – for possession
Where – for places
When – for time
What = "the thing that"

Defining Relative Clauses:

Fill in the blanks with the appropriate relative pronoun:

1) He's the man _____ I saw in the park last week.

2) That's the lady _____ vicious dog bit me.

3) It's a shop _____ sells trendy clothes.

4) That's the restaurant _____ we always go.

5) The customer _____ called this morning didn't leave a name.

6) This is the film _____ I saw at the cinema last week.

7) She's the woman _____ daughter is an ace pilot.

8) I still don't know _____ you mean.

9) Is that the book _____ you are reading?

10) That's the place _____ I work.

Non-defining Relative Clauses:

Correct the mistakes in the following sentences:

1) The room has a toilet and shower, that is very convenient.

2) Last month I saw my mother who is nearly 80.

3) London the biggest city in England is around 2000 years old.

4) The cat, who owner is 27, is black with white paws.

5) I visited my father, who he is twice my age.

6) My brother who is a plumber is married.

Use non-defining relative clauses to combine these sentences and pack in more information:

1) The teacher was an inspiration to his pupils. He was 48.

_____

2) The company is on the verge of collapse. Its headquarters are in Rio.

_____

3) The man was thin. He was gravely ill.

_____

4) The TV blew up. It was in the living room.

_____

5) The cat was hit by a car. It was black.

_____

Speaking Practice:

Complete these sentences with your partner and add more information:

1) I have been to a restaurant which…

2) I know a man who…

3) There is a place in my country where…

4) I saw someone whose house…

5) I know a shop which…

6) There is a TV programme in my country which…

7) I have a relative who…

8) There was a teacher in my school who…

9) I have a friend who…

10) There is a man whose…

11) I know a place where…

12) In my country there is a dish which…

13) I don't like people who…

14) I love people who…

15) I have a problem when…

16) There are many people who…

17) I like restaurants where…

18) I like food which…

19) I am happy when…

20) I like teachers who…

Extension – make at least 5 more sentences:

Unit 24: So and Such

When do you use 'so' and when do you use 'such'?

So + adjective
So + adverb
Such + noun
Such + noun phrase

Fill in the blanks with 'so' or 'such':

1) It was _____ humid that I nearly fainted.

2) Kevin is _____ a kind person to all who know him.

3) There was _____ turbulence in the plane that I felt queasy.

4) He ran _____ slowly that he had no chance at all of winning the marathon.

5) If you climb Mount Everest, the air can be _____ thin that breathing is difficult.

6) The view across the lush pastures was _____ beautiful it took my breath away.

7) We had _____ a lovely time with you yesterday.

8) My children had _____ fun in the park the other day.

9) When we took the ferry across the river, the crossing was _____ choppy that we felt scared.

10) I used to be _____ a timid boy when I was younger.

11) Time flies _____ quickly when you are older.

12) It was _____ a shame that he failed to pass the entrance exam.

13) Thanks _____ much for helping me move house yesterday!

14) Walking along the banks of the river can be _____ a pleasant way to spend the afternoon.

Speaking Practice

Put these questions and sentences in the right order and then ask your partner:

1) you/have/ever/sad/you/that/cried/felt/so?

2) such/you/time/was/last/the/when/had/fun?

3) nice/talk/again/about/can/a/place/you/that/wanted/so/you/was/to/go?

4) you/can/when/tired/time/so/a/you/remember/felt?

5) have/felt/so/shaking/that/you/you/ever/scared/were?

6) so/felt/about/talk/a/can/when/you/you/time/happy?

7) you/ever/big/had/hospital/a/pain/have/such/went/that/you/to?

8) the/time/were/cold/shivered/was/last/you/so/when/that/you?

9) time/you/about/a/you/talk/you/were/sweated/can/so/hot/that?

10) a/about/weather/when/talk/you/time/experienced/you/such/can/nice?

11) stomach/when/you/did/feel/so/last/rumbled/hungry/that/your?

12) about/you/can/talk/a/person/you/nice/time/met/such/a?

13) you/have/ever/was/food/that/bad/eaten/so?

14) happy/talk/can/about/had/a/such/you/when/you/a/time/day?

Extension – make at least 3 more questions to ask your partner:

Unit 25: The Passive

When/why do we use the passive?

What is the form?

Form: **Be + PP**

Tense	Active	Passive
Present simple	Eat	
Present continuous	Be eating	
Future (will)	Will eat	
Future (going to)	Be going to eat	
Past simple	Ate	
Past continuous	Was eating	
Present perfect	Has eaten	
Past perfect	Had eaten	
Infinitive (with 'to')	To eat	

Change the verb into the appropriate passive form and fill in the gaps:

1) My cake has gone! It _____ (eat).

2) The plane _____ by the Wright brothers (invent).

3) A man _____ by the police last night (arrest).

4) Several UFOs _____ flying over London recently (see).

5) A lot of cheese _____ in Holland (eat).

6) Spanish _____ in Argentina (speak).

7) My wallet _____. I'm going to the police station (steal).

8) The actor died when the film _____ (shoot).

9) At this moment many lessons _____ in Britain (teach).

10) In the future trips to Mars _____ using a spaceship (make).

11) The TV _____ in Britain (invent).

12) The door should only _____ in an emergency (open).

Speaking Practice

Speak about these topics with your partner using the passive:

Think of a film:

Where was it set?
When was it made?
Who was it directed by?
What country was it made by?
Was it dubbed or subtitled?

Think of a dish you have eaten:

Where was it first made?
How is it made?
When is it usually eaten?

Think of a book:

Who was it written by?
When was it set?
Where was it set?
When was it written?

Think of a game:

How is it played?
Where was it invented?
When was it invented?

Think of an invention:

Who was it invented by?
When was it invented?
Where was it invented?
What was it invented for?

Unit 26: Reported Speech

Can you give an example of reported speech?

How do verbs change in reported speech?

Direct Speech	Reported Speech
Present simple	Past simple
Present continuous	Past continuous
Will	Would
Is/are going to	Was/were going to
Past simple	Past perfect
Present perfect	Past perfect

Some modals change: *can > could; may > might; must > had to*; others stay the same: *could; might; should.*

Put the direct speech into reported speech:

Direct	Reported
1) "I swim well"	He said (that) he swam well.
2) "I am talking"	He..
3) "He will go"	He..
4) "She's going to pay"	She...
5) "I saw him in the pub"	He..
6) "I have been there"	He..
7) "They feel sick"	He..
8) "I can play the piano"	He..
9) "You should see a doctor"	He..
10) "I will be able to help"	He..
11) "I'm going to relax"	She...
12) "I must go now"	He..

Reported Questions:

Rules: 1) use "**if/whether**" for *yes/no* questions
2) word order: subject > verb
3) no auxiliary verbs

e.g. "What time is it?" > He asked what time it was.

Put the direct questions into reported questions:

Direct	Reported

He asked…

1) "Where do you live?"   ....

2) "Are you hungry?"   ....

3) "Where are you going?"   ....

4) "Have you been to Japan?"   ....

5) "Did you see Tom yesterday?"   ....

6) "Should we go home?"   ....

7) "Is Linda sick?"   ....

8) "How old are you?"   ....

9) "Can pigs fly?"   ....

10) "Must you go now?"   ....

11) "Does this bus go to London?"   ....

12) "Where are you going tonight?"   ....

13) "Could you help me?"   ....

14) "Did you have to go?"   ....

15) "Do you think you may come?"   ....

16) "What should you do for a cold?"   ....

Speaking Practice:

First, write questions to ask your partner. Then, ask your partner and write the answers briefly. Last, write the reported question and answer then tell a different partner:

Question	Answer	Reported Question & Answer

Unit 27: Reporting Verbs

What is a reporting verb? Can you think of any examples?

V-ing	to + inf.	person + to + inf.
Apologize for	Agree	Advise
Accuse sb of	Offer	Ask
Admit	Refuse	Convince
Blame sb for	Promise	Encourage
Deny	Threaten	Invite
Insist on		Persuade
Recommend		Remind
Regret		Tell
Suggest		Warn
(not) doing something	**(not) to do something**	**somebody (not) to do something**

Choose from the above verbs then add the verb at the end of the sentence:

1) The suspect totally _____ in court (lie).

2) Unfortunately, my boss _____ my salary (increase).

3) He really _____ the new restaurant in Bow Street (try).

4) Sue _____ Cathy _____ out alone at night (go).

5) I deeply _____ at school when I had the chance (study).

6) The man pulled a knife and _____ him unless he gave him the money (stab).

7) They kindly _____ me mow the lawn (help).

8) The man _____ the boy for _____ the window (break).

9) He _____ to the lady for _____ the vase (drop).

10) She _____ to lock the door next week (forget).

Speaking Practice

Fill in the gaps with the correct form of the verbs in brackets:

1) Where would you recommend _____ for a holiday in your country (go)?

2) What would you advise someone _____ to get over a cold (do)?

3) Is there a place in your country which you would warn people not _____ (visit)?

4) Where would you suggest _____ to eat out in a restaurant (go)?

5) Have you ever been accused of _____ anything you hadn't done (do)?

6) Have you ever agreed _____ anything you later regretted (do)?

7) When was the last time you apologised for _____ something wrong (do)?

8) Were there any teachers at school who encouraged you _____ hard (work)?

9) Has anyone ever threatened _____ you (harm)?

10) Do you often offer _____ people (help)?

11) When was the last time you refused _____ something (do)?

12) What do you regret _____ when you were younger (do)?

13) Have you ever admitted _____ a lie (tell)?

14) If you were served a substandard meal in a restaurant, would you refuse _____ for it (pay)?

Extension – make at least 3 more questions to ask your partner:

Unit 28: Definite Articles

When do you use the definite article?

Use *"the"*…

When there is only 1 of something
When there is one particular type of something
With adjectives
With nationalities
Playing musical instruments
Names with "of" in
Families
Countries with plurals
Names of rivers, seas, oceans, mountain ranges, pubs, hotels

Don't use *"the"*…

Countries and islands
Cities & towns
Street names
Mountains

Put the definite article in the spaces below where appropriate:

1) John can play _____ guitar beautifully.

2) _____ rich seldom share their wealth with _____ poor.

3) _____ potato was introduced to England by Sir Francis Drake.

4) _____ England is part of _____ UK.

5) _____ biggest river in _____ London is _____ Thames.

6) _____ Browns live in _____ Green Street.

7) My colleague visited _____ Jamaica in _____ Caribbean.

8) _____ Tower of London is in _____ central London.

9) _____ Sun rises in _____ east and sets in _____ west.

10) _____ Cabbage Patch is a pub in _____ Twickenham.

Speaking Practice

Add the definite article to these questions where necessary. Next, answer the questions with your partner and add something extra:

1) What is best place to visit in your country?

2) What is longest river in your country?

3) Can you play piano or guitar?

4) Have you ever visited Netherlands?

5) Do you know anyone who lives in United States?

6) What is your favourite country in Europe?

7) How much do unemployed get in your country?

8) Have you ever seen Eiffel Tower?

9) Do rich pay high taxes in your country?

10) What is name of city where you were born?

11) Have you ever swum in sea?

12) Do you ever go to pubs?

13) What is name of highest mountain in your country?

14) What is name of best hotel in your town/city?

15) Which nationality do you like most?

16) What is fastest animal in your country?

Unit 29: Prepositions

Prepositions of Time:

At	Clock times, points in day	At 9am, at noon, at night
	Holiday periods, points in time	At Easter, at the weekend, at the time, at the beginning
In	Parts of the day, months, years, seasons	In the morning, in May, in 1980, in spring
	For a time in the future	In 2 weeks, in an hour, in a moment
On	Specific days and dates	On Friday, On Christmas Day, on May 2nd, On New Year's Day, On Tuesday morning

Prepositions of Place:

At	Point where something happens	At the door
	Expressions	At school/work, at home, at the table, at university, at the top
In	Inside something	In the box
	Expressions	In bed, in the sky, in hospital, in the park, in a book, in the middle
On	Expressions	On the island, on TV, on Earth, on the beach, on the page, on a trip, on a mountain, on a farm

Fill in the gaps with the correct preposition:

I was _____ home _____ bed _____ Christmas Eve when suddenly _____ 9 o'clock _____ night I heard a knock _____ the door. It was my friend John who was studying _____ university. I opened the door and let him _____ my house. He told me that _____ three weeks he was going to teach _____ a school _____ an island _____ the Caribbean. He told me he wanted to lie _____ a famous beach he had seen _____ TV and sit _____ the beautiful sunshine. He stayed the night and _____ the morning he got up and left. I saw him off _____ the door and he waved goodbye as he was sitting _____ his cab.

Speaking Practice

Put the appropriate preposition into the gaps.
Next ask your partner and add more information:

1) What is the most beautiful place _____ Earth?

2) What is your favourite pastime _____ home?

3) What do you enjoy doing _____ night?

4) Is there anything you like doing _____ the morning?

5) What are you going to do _____ the weekend?

6) What do you do _____ New Year's Day in your country?

7) What is the best thing you have watched _____ TV?

8) What did you study _____ school/university in your country?

9) Have you ever sunbathed _____ a beach?

10) Have you ever been _____ an island?

11) How long do you lie _____ bed _____ the weekend?

12) What do you like doing _____ summer?

13) Where will you be _____ ten years' time?

14) When was the last time you were _____ hospital?

15) Have you ever been _____ a trip you really enjoyed?

16) Have you ever been _____ the newspaper or _____ TV?

17) Have you ever been _____ a farm?

18) Have you ever been _____ a mountain?

Unit 30: Used To

What's the difference between "I am used to living in London" and "I used to live in London"?

Used to + inf. – habit/state in past
Would + inf. – habit in past (esp. nostalgia)
Be used to + V-ing – you are accustomed to something
            + noun
Get used to + V-ing – you are *becoming* accustomed to something
            + noun

Use the correct form of the patterns above in the sentences below (some are negative):

1) There _____ an ice skating rink in Twickenham (be).

2) When I was young I _____ to the park and have picnics every summer (go).

3) I _____ the piano well but now I am really good (play).

4) Hiroko finds it difficult to _____ British cuisine.

5) Tom will have to _____ early in the mornings (get up).

6) I _____ timid but now I'm more self-confident (be).

7) Thomas _____ on the left side of the road yet (drive).

8) He is finally _____ in the UK (live).

9) Fred found it hard to _____ the humidity in Tokyo.

10) As Rob _____ nightshift, he fell asleep on the job (work).

11) Janet soon _____ chopsticks when she lived in China (use).

12) Sue had to leave the party as she _____ so badly (treat).

Speaking Practice

Correct the mistakes in these questions then ask your partner:

1) Where did you used to live as a child?

2) Do you have any happy memories of anything you would to do as a child?

3) Are you used to speak and think in English?

4) Is there anything you found difficult to get use to?

5) What did you used be like as a child?

6) Where did you used to go as a teenager?

7) Did you used to smoke when you were younger?

8) Is there anything you are still not use to?

9) Did you used to do more exercise in the past?

10) What job did you used to want to do as a child?

11) How old were you when you get used to ride a bike?

12) Did you used to like living in your country?

Extension - make at least 5 more questions to ask your partner:

Unit 31: Phrasal Verbs – Get

Get on with = have a good relationship
Get by = have just enough of something
Get up to = do something (usually negative)
Get someone down = make someone sad
Get to someone = make someone annoyed
Get out of something = avoid doing something
Get over = recover from
Get round to = finally do something
Get around = spread
Get off = avoid being punished

Fill in the gaps below with the correct form of the phrasal verb:

1) When I was young and poor, it was hard to _____.

2) Drinking hot lemon juice is one way to _____ a cold.

3) Although he likes his sister, he _____ his older brother.

4) News quickly _____ that the two boys had been found guilty of trespassing on the farm.

5) It was clear that he had committed the crime but he_____ on a technicality.

6) When I was young and reckless, I _____ a lot of trouble.

7) Sue can't find a suitable job; it really _____ her.

8) Edward was always busy and he couldn't _____ finishing his work.

9) Kenny is bone idle and always does his best to _____ doing work.

10) Mike became very unhappy at work as he did not think it was a safe place to work and no one appreciated his work ethic. This really _____.

Speaking Practice

Put the words in the correct order. Then practise with your partner.

1) in/do/best/with/who/you/on/get/your/family?

2) much/you/get/how/to/every/money/do/need/by/month/from/job/a?

3) did/use/bad/were/when/you/up/to/to/get/anything/you/younger?

4) is/anything/there/gets/down/that/you/your/job/about?

5) there/anything/is/that/you/gets/to?

6) anything/is/there/that/would/rather/out/you/of/get/doing?

7) over/is/what/way/good/a/get/to/stress/work/at?

8) how/get/you/do/often/to/round/English/learning?

9) what/of/news/kind/gets/fast/around?

10) you/got/ever/have/off/anything?

Extension – write at least 5 questions using the above phrasal verbs to ask your partner:

Unit 32: Phrasal Verbs – Go

Go up = increase

Go ahead = start doing something planned

Go through = experience

Go without = not have something

Go down with = become sick with

Go off = become bad

Go on = continue

Go out with = have a relationship with

Go with = suit

Go for = choose

Fill in the gaps below with the correct form of the phrasal verb:

1) My blue jacket _____ my green shirt so I took it back to the shop.

2) Kim and Jim have been _____ each other for over a year.

3) After sitting outside in the rain he _____ a cold.

4) The prices in shops seem to _____ every year.

5) As Bill had lost his family, he found it hard to _____ with the future.

6) In World War 2 many people _____ great hardships.

7) In warm weather meat can easily _____ so it's best to refrigerate it as soon as possible.

8) She had two choices but she _____ the cheaper option.

9) He _____ with his decision to buy a new property last year.

10) Sally didn't have enough money so she had to _____ her little luxuries.

Speaking Practice

Put the words in the correct order. Then practise with your partner.

1) you/anything/go/have/ever/to/had/without?

2) you/with/do/have/plans/to/ahead/any/you/that/want/go?

3) you/gone/know/anyone/through/do/experience/has/who/a/bad

4) prices/are/much/how/up/going/by/country/your/in?

5) was/went/when/with/time/an/last/the/down/illness/you?

6) that/gone/you/have/ever/food/eaten/off/had?

7) it/have/you/ever/found/something/hard/with/go/to/on?

8) the/to/best/age/with/when/is/out/go/someone?

9) go/with/best/kind/of/clothes/what/you?

10) choice/you/for/what/of/kind/had/if/you/restaurant/would/go/the?

Extension – write at least 5 questions using the above phrasal verbs to ask your partner:

Answer Key

Unit 1 – Present Simple

1) loves 2) meets 3) doesn't sleep 4) travels 5) doesn't like 6) look 7) serves 8) cooks 9) think 10) drinks 11) feels 12) don't work 13) starts 14) studies 15) doesn't drive

1) What do you do every day? 2) What time do you get up every morning? 3) What time do you go to bed? 4) How often do you use a computer? 5) Where do you go shopping? 6) Do you take a bath or shower at night? 7) How do you relax when you are tired? 8) How often do you go out to eat in a restaurant? 9) How do you get to school or work? 10) What do you eat and drink every day? 11) How often do you meet your friends? 12) What do you do when you meet your friends? 13) Who do you meet most often? 14) What do you like doing on holiday? 15) What do you like doing when you are free?

Unit 2 – Present Continuous

1) is raining 2) are...doing 3) is crying 4) is shaking 5) am feeling 6) are...irritating 7) is working 8) am meeting 9) aren't studying 10) isn't working 11) are...taking 12) is ringing 13) isn't improving 14) is working 15) is growing 16) is running 17) is doing 18) isn't shining

1) What are you doing now? 2) Where are you living now? 3) Where are you going next weekend? 4) Who are you meeting next week? 5) What is your friend doing now? 6) Where are you going for your next holiday? 7) Where is your friend living now? 8) What are you eating tonight? 9) Where is your friend working at the moment? 10) What are you thinking about at the moment?

Unit 3 – Present Simple & Present Continuous

1) is watching 2) is meeting 3) loves 4) commutes 5) isn't raining 6) look 7) is drinking 8) starts 9) think 10) is thinking 11) feels 12) is cooking

1) What do you usually do on Saturday nights? 2) How do you usually spend your weekends? 3) How often do you go out to eat in a restaurant? 4) What are you doing now? 5) Where are you going tomorrow? 6) How do you travel to school or work? 7) How often do you meet your friends? 8) What book are you reading at the moment? 9) Are you participating in any clubs or activities at the moment? 10) Are you learning how to do anything at the moment?

Unit 4 – Past

1) watched 2) didn't clean 3) didn't start 4) cooked 5) Did...study 6) climbed 7) visited 8) didn't wash 9) Did...dance 10) listened 11) relaxed 12) didn't play

Verb	Past	Verb	Past	Verb	Past	Verb	Past
Buy	*Bought*	Go	*Went*	Make	*Made*	Sleep	*Slept*
Can	*Could*	Have	*Had*	Meet	*Met*	Speak	*Spoke*
Do	*Did*	Is	*Was/were*	Pay	*Paid*	Stand	*Stood*

Drink	*Drank*	Know	*Knew*	Read	*Read*	Take	*Took*
Eat	*Ate*	Leave	*Left*	See	*Saw*	Write	*Wrote*

1) went 2) drank 3) ate 4) wrote 5) spoke 6) met 7) bought 8) left 9) saw 10) paid 11) stood 12) read 13) took 14) did

1) were 2) were 3) wasn't 4) weren't 5) was 6) was 7) wasn't 8) weren't 9) were 10) wasn't 11) wasn't 12) wasn't 13) weren't 14) Was

Unit 5 – Past Continuous

1) was snowing 2) were playing 3) was eating 4) were wearing 5) was exercising 6) was standing 7) wasn't raining 8) was running 9) was walking 10) was travelling 11) wasn't looking 12) was sitting 13) weren't concentrating 14) was making

Unit 6 – Question Forms

1) Where are you from?/Where do you come from? 2) Where do you live now? 3) What is your hobby? 4) How often do you play? 5) Are you married? 6) Do you have (any) children? 7) How old are they? 8) What does your wife do? 9) Does she like her job? 10) How often does she work?

1) Where do you live? 2) Do you like where you live? 3) Where did you live before? 4) When were you born? 5) Where were you born? 6) What do you do? 7) How do you get to school or work? 8) Are you married? 9) Do you have any children? 10) How many brothers and sisters do you have? 11) Who do you like best in your family? 12) Who is your best friend? 13) What is your hobby? 14) How often do you (do) exercise? 15) What did you do last weekend? 16) Who did you meet last weekend?

1) What do you do? 2) How old are you? 3) How long have you lived here? 4) How long have you been learning English? 5) What's your favourite food? 6) What (kind of) music do you like listening to? 7) Who is your best friend? 8) How would your friends describe you? 9) What is your dream? 10) What makes you happy?

Unit 7 – Indirect Questions

1) where the bank is? 2) who you are? 3) why he was late? 4) where you were? 5) what that is? 6) how I can do it? 7) if you were early? 8) how much it is? 9) if you did it? 10) what you saw? 11) where he lives? 12) who you met? 13) if you are satisfied? 14) if he met him?

1) Can you tell me where the nearest train station is? 2) Can you inform me how to get to the station? 3) Do you know where the best place to eat in your city is? 4) Do you know a good way to make money? 5) Do you have any idea who the richest man in the world is? 6) Can you tell me about where you live? 7) Could you tell me a good way to get a (good) job? 8) Would you tell me about when you were a child? 9) Do you know how much a house (in your country) costs in your country? 10) Could you tell me what the best place in your country is? 11) Would you mind informing me what a good way to learn English is? 12) Could you tell me how long you are going to live in this country?

Unit 8 – Present Perfect

1) has taken 2) met 3) forgot 4) has lived 5) has grown 6) haven't had 7) has gone 8) has known 9) found 10) have forgotten 11) went 12) was; has been stolen.

1) What have you done today? 2) How long have you lived here for? 3) What have you done just before the lesson? 4) How long have you known your best friend for? 5) Have you already eaten today? 6) What is the most expensive thing you have bought in your whole life? 7) What is the most exciting thing you have ever done in your life? 8) What is the best film you have ever seen? 9) Who is the strangest person you have ever met? 10) Where is the most beautiful place you have ever visited? 11) What is the best food you have ever eaten? 12) What is the best birthday present you have ever received? 13) Where is the best place you have been to in your country? 14) Can you talk about a place which you have not been to yet?

Unit 9 – Present Perfect Continuous

1) have been studying 2) has been playing 3) have...been doing 4) has written 5) have been drinking 6) has been suffering 7) have played 8) has drunk 9) have been going out
10) Have...been crying 11) has been cleaned 12) has fixed

1) a hobby that you have been doing for a long time. 2) how long you have been learning English. 3) how long you have been living here. 4) an establishment that you have been frequenting for a long time. 5) a TV programme you have been following. 6) a kind of music you have been listening to. 7) a good friend you have been visiting. 8) a shop you have been going to for a while. 9) a book that you have been reading. 10) how long you have been doing your job.

Unit 10 – Past Perfect

1) had left 2) had gone 3) had died 4) slept 5) had left 6) had played 7) had left 8) saw
9) hadn't met 10) had fallen 11) dropped 12) hadn't started

Unit 11 – Future

1) will turn on 2) are going to win 3) am working 4) is going to watch 5) will answer 6) is going to sink 7) will call 8) is leaving 9) am going to wear 10) going to fall 11) will be 12) will give

1) What are you doing tomorrow? 2) What are you going to do at the weekend? 3) What time are you going to get up tomorrow? 4) When are you going to go shopping next? 5) Do you think you will ever marry a foreigner? 6) Who do you think will win the next World Cup? 7) What is the next place you are going to visit? 8) What are you going to do after class? 9) Do you think you will ever become wealthy? 10) How are you going to spend your next summer holiday? 11) What do you think the weather will be like tomorrow? 12) Who is the next person you are going to meet?

Unit 12 – Narratives

1) was raining 2) rained 3) thought 4) was thinking 5) slept 6) was sleeping 7) cried 8) was crying 9) stood 10) were standing

1) had worked/had been working 2) had worked/had been working 3) had been stealing 4) had eaten 5) had been raining 6) had been cooking 7) had been playing 8) had been sitting 9) had broken 10) had been stolen

woke; had been raining; left; took; was leaving; realised; had forgotten; got; returned; got; looked; remembered; had given; took; had forgotten; had given; arrived; had…left.

Unit 13 – Future Continuous & Future Perfect

1) will be doing 2) will have finished 3) will be visiting 4) will be working/will have worked 5) will have travelled 6) will have been cleaned 7) will be living 8) will have seen 9) will be sunbathing 10) will have finished 11) will have been 12) will be enjoying 13) Will…be staying 14) won't have completed

Unit 14 – Comparatives & Superlatives

1) bigger 2) further 3) more interesting 4) worse 5) worst 6) healthier 7) not as hard 8) better 9) as far 10) most boring 11) more dangerous 12) the most intelligent 13) not as fast 14) more precious

Unit 15 – Modals of Obligation and Advice

1) had to wear 2) should take 3) must go 4) have to finish 5) must be 6) shouldn't leave 7) must visit 8) must leave 9) had to study 10) should take 11) don't have to wear 12) didn't have to pay

Unit 16 – Modals of Deduction

1) can't be 2) must be 3) might/could be 4) must be 5) might/could be 6) might/could be 7) can't be 8) might/could be 9) can't be 10) might/could be 11) must be 12) might/could be 13) must be 14) can't be

1) False – the most common name is Mohammed (with many different spellings) 2) False – it is Finland 3) True 4) True 5) False – Qatar is the richest per head 6) True – humans expand and contract very slightly throughout the day 7) False – it is Japan 8) True – your nails and hair continue to grow for a short period 9) True – she has her real birthday and an official birthday in June 10) False – it is Jupiter 11) True 12) True 13) True 14) False – it is Mexico 15) False – it is an Afghan hound 16) True 17) True – they ask more than 100 18) True – named so by the Romans

Unit 17 – Gerunds & Infinitives

1) to relax 2) drinking 3) Eating 4) to go 5) walking 6) trying 7) Keeping 8) to eat 9) to study 10) drinking 11) getting 12) to get 13) to buy 14) to meet

1) to do 2) doing 3) learning 4) speaking 5) to come 6) to go 7) getting 8) going 9) doing 10) sleeping 11) keeping 12) to do 13) doing 14) going 15) to improve 16) to do

Unit 18 – Conditionals

1) jump, will die 2) resign, doesn't get 3) rains, will get 4) opens, push 5) win, will buy 6) heat, boils 7) hurry, will miss 8) stroke, will scratch 9) blush, compliment 10) study, will pass

1) were, would fly 2) were, would buy 3) would be, wore 4) had done, would have got 5) had, would buy 6) had known, would have resigned 7) would be, lived 8) had arrived, would have seen 9) hadn't met, wouldn't have been 10) was stolen, would notify

1) What would you do if you won a lot of money? 2) Where will you go if you go on holiday this year? 3) What will you do if it snows tomorrow? 4) What would you do if you spoke better English? 5) What would you do if your friend got into trouble? 6) What do you do if it's sunny? 7) What would you do if you could travel to the moon? 8) What do you do if someone pays you a compliment? 9) What would you have done if you had been born 1,000 years ago? 10) What would you do if your wallet was stolen? 11) What do you do if someone of the opposite sex smiles at you? 12) Where would you go if you ever emigrated?

Unit 19 – Mixed Conditionals

1) had worked, would be 2) wouldn't be, had missed/would be, hadn't missed 3) was, would have got 4) was, would have made 5) hadn't forgotten, wouldn't be/had forgotten, would be 6) wouldn't be, hadn't broken down 7) hadn't spent, wouldn't be 8) was, would have won 9) was, would have passed 10) wouldn't be, hadn't met 11) wouldn't be, hadn't eaten 12) was, would have got

1) Where would you be now if you hadn't come here? 2) What would you be doing now if you had studied English harder? 3) How would life be different if you had been born poor? 4) How would you feel if you were one metre taller? 5) What would you have done if you were more clever? 6) What would you have done if you were invisible? 7) How would your life be different if you had broken both legs? 8) What would you have cooked me if you were a good cook? 9) If you had lost all your money, who would you ask for help? 10) How would your life be different if you had won the lottery?

Unit 20 – Wish/If Only

1) I wish I didn't live in London 2) I wish I wasn't working tomorrow 3) I wish I wasn't going to meet my boss 4) I wish I had studied at school 5) I wish I hadn't left my girlfriend 6) I wish I hadn't been cooking all day 7) I wish I hadn't broken my leg 8) I wish I wasn't going to be 40 next birthday 9) I wish I hadn't lost my job 10) I wish my car hadn't been stolen 11) I wish my computer wasn't broken 12) I wish people listened to me

Unit 21 – Have Something Done

1) going to have it cleaned. 2) going to it painted. 3) going to have it fixed. 4) going to have…pierced. 5) has had her hair cut. 6) had it repaired 7) has had it stolen. 8) had…searched. 9) having…taken 10) had it installed 11) had…blown down. 12) had it made.

1) Where do you usually have your hair cut? 2) Do you mind having your photo taken? 3) When was the last time you had your photo taken? 4) Have you ever had your money stolen? 5) Have you ever had a cake made? 6) Have you had your ears pierced? 7) Have you ever had anything repaired? 8) Do you ever have your clothes dry cleaned? 9) Do you fix your house yourself or have it repaired by someone? 10) Have you ever had a part of your body broken? 11) When was the last time you had your homework checked? 12) Have you ever had your phone broken?

Unit 22 – Quantifiers

1) much 2) a little 3) a lot of 4) plenty of 5) many 6) a few 7) plenty of 8) many 9) a lot of 10) a lot of 11) a little 12) a few 13) much 14) a little 15) few 16) a little

Countable	Uncountable	Both
sweets, vegetables, games, movies, dramas, game shows	water, alcohol, coffee, meat, bread, junk food, wholemeal food, fruit, rice, health food	fish, TV, sport, exercise

Unit 23 – Relative Clauses

1) who 2) whose 3) which 4) where 5) who 6) which 7) whose 8) what 9) which 10) where

1) The room has a toilet and shower, ~~that~~ which is very convenient. 2) Last month I saw my mother, who is nearly 80. 3) London, the biggest city in England, is around 2000 years old. 4) The cat, ~~who~~ whose owner is 27, is black with white paws. 5) I visited my father, who ~~he~~ is twice my age. 6) My brother, who is a plumber, is married.

1) The teacher, who was 48, was an inspiration to his pupils. 2) The company, whose headquarters are in Rio, is on the verge of collapse. 3) The man, who was thin, was gravely ill. 4) The TV, which was in the living room, blew up. 5) The cat, which was black, was hit by a car.

Unit 24 – So & Such

1) so 2) such 3) such 4) so 5) so 6) so 7) such 8) such 9) so 10) such 11) so 12) such 13) so 14) such

1) Have you ever felt so sad that you cried? 2) When was the last time you had such fun? 3) Can you talk about a place that was so nice you wanted to go again? 4) Can you remember a time when you felt so tired? 5) Have you ever felt so scared that you were shaking? 6) Can you talk about a time when you felt so happy? 7) Have you ever had such a big pain that you

went to hospital? 8) When was the last time you were so cold that you shivered? 9) Can you talk about a time that you were so hot you sweated? 10) Can you talk about a time when you experienced such nice weather? 11) When did you last feel so hungry that your stomach rumbled? 12) Can you talk about a time you met such a nice person? 13) Have you ever eaten food that was so bad? 14) Can you talk about a time when you had such a happy day?

Unit 25 – Passive

is/are eaten, is/are being eaten, will be eaten, is/are going to be eaten, was/were eaten, was/were being eaten, has/have been eaten, had been eaten, to be eaten

1) has been eaten 2) was invented 3) was arrested 4) have been seen 5) is eaten 6) is spoken 7) has been stolen 8) was being shot 9) are being taught 10) will be made 11) was invented 12) be opened

Unit 26 – Reported Speech

2) He said that he was talking 3) He said that he would go 4) She said that she was going to pay 5) He said he had seen him in the pub 6) He said that he had been there 7) He said that they felt sick 8) He said that he could play the piano 9) He said that I should see a doctor 10) He said that he would be able to help 11) She said that she was going to relax 12) He said that he had to go now

1) He asked where I lived 2) He asked if I was hungry 3) He asked where I was going 4) He asked if I had been to Japan 5) He asked if I had seen Tom yesterday/the day before 6) He asked if they should go home 7) He asked if Linda was sick 8) He asked how old I was 9) He asked if pigs could fly 10) He asked if I had to go now 11) He asked if this bus went to London 12) He asked where I was going tonight/that night 13) He asked if I could help him 14) He asked if I had to go 15) He asked if I thought I might come 16) He asked what I should do for a cold

Unit 27 – Reporting Verbs

1) denied lying 2) refused to increase 3) recommended trying 4) warned…not to go 5) regret not studying 6) threatened to stab 7) offered to help 8) blamed…breaking 9) apologised…dropping 10) promised not to forget

1) going 2) to do 3) to visit 4) going 5) doing 6) to do 7) doing 8) to work 9) to harm 10) to help 11) to do 12) doing 13) telling 14) to pay

Unit 28 – Definite Articles

1) the 2) The…the 3) The 4) No article…the 5) The…no article…the 6) The…no article 7) No article…the 8) The…no article 9) The…the…the 10) The…no article

1) What is best the place to visit in your country? 2) What is the longest river in your country? 3) Can you play the piano or the guitar? 4) Have you ever visited the Netherlands? 5) Do you know anyone who lives in the United States? 6) What is your favourite country in Europe? 7) How much do the unemployed get in your country? 8) Have you ever seen the Eiffel Tower? 9) Do the rich pay high taxes in your country? 10) What is the name of the city

where you were born? 11) Have you ever swum in the sea? 12) Do you ever go to pubs? 13) What is the name of the highest mountain in your country? 14) What is the name of the best hotel in your town/city? 15) Which nationality do you like the most? 16) What is the fastest animal in your country?

Unit 29 – Prepositions

at; in; on; at; at; at; at; in; in; at; on; in; on; on; in; in; at; in

1) on 2) at 3) at 4) in 5) at 6) on 7) on 8) at 9) on 10) on 11) in...at 12) in 13) in 14) in 15) on 16) in...on 17) on 18) on

Unit 30 – Used to

1) used to be 2) would go 3) didn't use to play 4) get used to 5) get used to getting up 6) used to be 7) isn't used to driving 8) used to living 9) get used to 10) wasn't used to working 11) got used to using 12) wasn't used to being treated

1) Where did you use to live as a child? 2) Do you have any happy memories of anything you would do as a child? 3) Are you used to speaking and thinking in English? 4) Is there anything you found difficult to get used to? 5) What did you use to be like as a child? 6) Where did you use to go as a teenager? 7) Did you use to smoke when you were younger? 8) Is there anything you are still not used to? 9) Did you use to do more exercise in the past? 10) What job did you use to want to do as a child? 11) How old were you when you got used to riding a bike? 12) Did you use to like living in your country?

Unit 31 – Phrasal Verbs - Get

1) get buy 2) get over 3) doesn't get on with 4) got around 5) got off 6) got into 7) gets to 8) get around to 9) get out of 10) got him down.

1) Who do you get on with best in your family? 2) How much do you need to get by every month from a job? 3) Did you use to get up to anything bad when you were younger? 4) Is there anything that gets you down about your job? 5) Is there anything that gets to you? 6) Is there anything that you would rather get out of doing? 7) What is a good way to get over stress at work? 8) How often do you get round to learning English? 9) What kind of news gets around fast? 10) Have you ever got off anything?

Unit 32 – Phrasal Verbs - Go

1) go off 2) going out 3) went down with 4) go up 5) go on 6) went through 7) didn't go with 8) went for 9) went ahead 10) go without

1) Have you ever had to go without anything? 2) Do you have any plans that you want to go ahead with? 3) Do you know anyone who has gone through a bad experience? 4) How much are prices going up by in your country? 5) When was the last time you went down with an illness? 6) Have you ever eaten food that had gone off? 7) Have you ever found it hard to go on with something? 8) When is the best age to go out with someone? 9) What

kind of clothes go with you best? 10) What kind of restaurant would you go for if you had the choice?

Verb Forms

Infinitive	Past	Past Participle
be	was/were	been
beat	beat	beaten
become	became	become
begin	began	begun
bite	bit	bitten
break	broke	broken
bring	brought	brought
build	built	built
buy	bought	bought
can	could	could
catch	caught	caught
choose	chose	chosen
come	came	come
cost	cost	cost
do	did	done
drink	drank	drunk
drive	drove	driven
eat	ate	eaten
fall	fell	fallen
feed	fed	fed
feel	felt	felt
fight	fought	fought
find	found	found
fly	flew	flown
forget	forgot	forgotten
get	got	got
give	gave	given
go	went	been/gone
grow	grew	grown
have	had	had
hear	heard	heard
hit	hit	hit
hold	held	held
hurt	hurt	hurt

Infinitive	Past	Past Participle
know	knew	known
learn	learnt	learnt
leave	left	left
lend	lent	lent
lose	lost	lost
make	made	made
mean	meant	meant
meet	met	met
pay	paid	paid
put	put	put
read	read	read
ride	rode	ridden
ring	rang	rung
run	ran	run
say	said	said
see	saw	seen
sell	sold	sold
send	sent	sent
sing	sang	sung
sit	sat	sat
sleep	slept	slept
speak	spoke	spoken
spend	spent	spent
stand	stood	stood
steal	stole	stolen
swim	swam	swum
take	took	taken
teach	taught	taught
tell	told	told
think	thought	thought
wake	woke	woken
wear	wore	worn
win	won	won
write	wrote	written

Printed in Great Britain
by Amazon

22135071R00051